Juneteenth!

Celebrating Freedom in Texas

By
Anna Pearl Barrett

EAKIN PRESS ⬥ Austin, Texas

Published in the United States of America
By Eakin Press
A Division of Sunbelt Media, Inc.
P.O. Box 90159 ★ Austin, TX 78709-0159
email: eakinpub@sig.net
www.eakinpress.com

3 4 5 6 7 8 9

1-57168-180-0

Library of Congress Cataloging-in-Publication Data

Barrett, Anna Pearl
    Juneteenth!: Celebrating Freedom in Texas / written by Anna Pearl
Barrett.
        p.   cm.
    Includes glossary.
    ISBN 1-57168-180-0
    1. Barrett, Anna Pearl—Childhood and youth. 2. Afro-Americans—
Texas—Galveston—Social life and customs. 3. Juneteenth—Texas—
Galveston. 4. Afro-Americans—Texas—Galveston—Biography. 5. Barrett
family—Biography. 6. Galveston (Tex.)—Biography.
    I. Title
F394.G2B35   1999
394.263—dc21   97-50513
                                                         CIP

Contents

1

Beginnings

"Eddie, I calculate that this Juneteenth is gonna make it eighty years since our people were set free! I reckon this year's freedom celebration ought to be the biggest one we ever had! I suspect that's how Ma and Pa'd want it, don't you?" Uncle Porter made his declaration to Daddy one fine evening in early May, while the two brothers and some of the children sat around on the front porch.

It was 1945. On this small Southeast Texas farm, the family always celebrated Juneteenth. The holiday celebrated June 19, 1865, the day that General Granger arrived in Galveston with the news about freedom for the slaves of Texas. President Lincoln had signed the Emancipation Proclamation, freeing the slaves throughout the

United States, two and a half years earlier. The children in the family always asked why it had taken so long for the news to get to Texas. Uncle Porter always answered, "Texas is a mighty big place! Why, there ain't another state big as ours, and if the truth be known, a whole lot of countries ain't big as Texas! Takes time to travel 'round all this land! The only thing that matters is that he got here!"

Juneteenth! A celebration of freedom and liberty, a day of great joy and jubilation in cities, towns, and hamlets throughout Texas. A true holiday long before the Texas Legislature made it official in 1979. It was always a wonderful fun-filled day with lots of family, friends, and history, so that generations of black people would remember the struggles and triumphs of their enslaved ancestors.

It was Uncle Porter who told the children about the family's history. "The reason I keep telling y'all 'bout the slavery time, and the hard row Pa and them had to hoe, is so y'all know and understand 'bout our history. That way y'all can see what kind of stock y'all spring from! That's important. I don't want to hear nothing 'bout y'all wasting time hating them slaver folks. What we want to do is celebrate what we done and work on making sure that y'all do better!"

Daddy and Uncle Porter and Momma and

everybody else in the family worked at a frenzied pace, preparing everything for the eightieth Juneteenth Freedom Celebration, to make it the finest one the family had ever had.

The first thing that Momma did was to start figuring out what the younger children would wear. Money was dear in big families in the 1940s, and there was not a lot to be spent on fancy clothes. Momma was a genius when it came to stretching a dollar, making ends meet, and creating original designs for her children to wear. "Just 'cause we don't have a lot of spare money for store-bought don't mean my young-uns got to look shabby," she always said.

She used twenty-five-pound flour sacks to make Annie and Neecie dresses. The sacks came in lovely flowered prints. Momma made sure when it was time to buy flour that she'd purchase a sack that matched one she already had. In those days families bought flour in such big bags because they made everything at home: biscuits, pies, muffins, pancakes, even stews and gravies. They kept the flour stored in a ten-gallon can with a tight lid on it.

For the dresses Momma would take the big hems of the white sheets that had worn out in the middle and would use the big hems that were still perfectly good to make pretty double ruffles on the dresses. She would sew on the recycled sheet hem ruffle and take a strip of the recycled flour sacks to make a top ruffle. Then she would sew both of the ruffles around the bottoms of the dresses and add a lovely expanse of ribbon or rickrack, which the Watkins salesman would have tucked away in his bag of goodies for her. The girls would end up with an original Suwillow creation that couldn't be beat. "Can't nobody hold a candle to them clothes your Momma whips up," Daddy voiced with pride.

Once Momma made Annie and Neecie's dresses, she set about whipping up something for Pelton and Royce. She cut down khaki pants and white dress shirts that Daddy and the older boys could no longer wear. She turned frayed collars and cuffs, took off sleeves, and cut down the shirts to fit Pelton and Royce. "Once we get these clothes starched and ironed, y'all gonna be the handsomest men at the celebration," she said.

Momma insisted that the children wear nice clothes. "Even if I have to work my fingers to the bones!" she declared as she zipped along on the old pedal sewing machine that she had inherited from Grandma Anne.

In those days not many mothers worked outside the home. They labored until they were bone-tired raising the children, cooking the family's meals, making the children's clothes, and making the lunches for family members going to work or to school. They taught the children to read and write, how to talk to adults, how to behave in public, and how to have pride in themselves and their accomplishments.

As Momma rightfully pointed out, "You just have to train the twigs the way you want them to grow, and they'll always bring glory to the family, instead of shame!"

2

A Big Surprise

As soon as school was out for the summer, Momma put Annie, Pelton, Neecie, and Royce to weeding and cleaning out the flower beds. Then they watered the seedlings they had transplanted from where the plants had gotten too thick. "When that chore's done Momma wants y'all to paint the rocks. We want everything to look nice when the rest of the family congregates for Juneteenth, don't we?" she asked.

"We want everything to look nice," Neecie imitated Momma.

"I hate all this hard old work. That's the one bad thing 'bout the celebration. It's so much work to do!" whined Annie.

"Now I know how poor old Grandpa Harrison and Grandma Anne felt when they had to work like slaves!" complained Pelton.

"Ain't no need in y'all carrying on so. The work's gotta be done, might as well just go on and do it," Royce observed.

"Look who's talking! That's just 'cause he ain't big enough to be much use!" Neecie snapped.

"Look who's talking! You may be older than Royce, but he's bigger than you!" Pelton snapped right back.

"And ain't neither one of y'all worth a hill of beans!" Annie couldn't stand to be left out of the argument.

"You young-uns stop all that squabbling! Here, come in out of the sun and rest. I got some peanut butter sandwiches and lemonade for you!" Momma called out to the bickering children.

The youngsters threw down their hoes and shovels and went flying to the front porch where Momma had put the plate of sandwiches and the pitcher of lemonade with glasses.

"Daddy's gonna fix the whitewash this evening, so y'all can start painting tomorrow," Momma said, smiling as she went back in the house to the groans of the children.

Most of the flower beds were cleaned out and ready for the whitewashed rocks to be placed around them. The crepe myrtles, oleanders, and wisteria had all been trimmed back, and where the children couldn't reach, Momma stopped her sewing, cooking, or canning and did it for them.

The children rested for a while after their lunch, but then Annie said, "Come on, y'all, we get the weeds out of Momma's day lilies and we'll be through!"

"But we'll just be through with the weeding and digging! We still got all that painting to do!" Neecie offered as a reality check.

That evening when Daddy came home, he had two big sacks of lime. One of the cousins had driven him up to the feed store in town to buy it. He would mix the lime with water to make the whitewash, for the children to whitewash the trees, all the rocks around Momma's flowers, and the hundreds of pickets surrounding the acre of land on which Daddy had built the house.

The children's complaints grew louder and stronger.

"*O-o-o-h* Lord have mercy! We ain't never gonna get through. We're gonna be painting till the day we die!"

"It's these old pickets! They're the worst thing in the world to try to paint!"

"The worst thing is you gotta paint both sides of 'em!"

"Painting the tree trunks ain't so bad!" said Royce, slopping his brush, sopping wet with whitewash, up and down a tree.

"That's 'cause Momma won't let you and Neecie paint the pickets. She knows me 'n Annie can do the best job. Y'all slop paint all over everything. Look at what a neat job we're doing!" said Pelton, lording his and Annie's superior ability over Royce and Neecie.

"No such thing! No such thing, Pelton! Me 'n Royce can paint just as good as you and Annie, any day of the week! There's too much water in this old whitewash, that's why it's such a mess! Humph! It's not our fault!" Neecie came right back at Pelton.

The four children whined and complained and painted until Momma called them in to eat lunch and rest for a while on the front porch. That was when she told them about the surprise that Daddy was planning for them. "What kind of surprise?" they wanted to know.

"You'll see!" Momma answered mysteriously.

"Momma's just fooling us. Daddy brings us a surprise every day when he comes home!" Neecie declared, referring to the piece of sandwich, muffin, or other treat that Daddy brought home every day in his lunch kit.

"No, it's not the little surprise from his lunch that he brings y'all. This is something special! It's gonna be here in time for the Juneteenth for everyone to enjoy, on account of y'all being such hard working children," proclaimed Momma.

Momma and Daddy had been squirreling away a little money each week to buy a radio. This was a major purchase for a family of humble means. Nobody bought "on time" in those days; that was living beyond your means.

The children plodded along with their whitewashing, whining, and complaining, until about a week before Juneteenth. That Friday evening Daddy was later getting home than usual. As he walked in the door he was carrying a big box.

"It must be the surprise!" The children went running to meet Daddy, just as they did every evening when they wanted to see what he had saved from lunch. This evening they paid no attention to the lunch pail.

"THE SURPRISE! THE SURPRISE! WHAT IS IT, DADDY?!" they shouted, grabbing at the big box.

"Now, now! You young-uns settle down. Here! Take the lunch box, I'll carry the surprise," Daddy said, chuckling.

The children *o-o-o-hed* and *a-a-a-hed* over the fine radio. Daddy plugged it in. "Your Momma will turn on this radio if she finds something she wants y'all to listen to. Otherwise y'all listen to it when we do, you hear?" Daddy said gravely.

On Saturday mornings about ten o'clock, after Annie and Neecie had cleaned up the kitchen and mopped the floor, Momma let them listen to *Let's Pretend* and *A Date With*

Judy. The Cream of Wheat commercial became their favorite song:

> *Oh, Cream of Wheat*
> *is so good to eat,*
> *if you have it every day*
> *it will make you strong,*
> *when you sing this song,*
> *it will make you shout Hurrah!*

In the evenings Momma would turn on the radio and they would listen to *Amos 'n Andy* or *The Shadow,* and on Saturday nights they could listen to *The Grand Old Opry*. Daddy loved that show and the children especially enjoyed hearing Cousin Minnie Pearl say, "I'm so proud to be here!"

During the day Annie and Neecie went around singing the Cream of Wheat song. They whined and complained about oatmeal, how hard they worked, and how if Momma and Daddy really cared anything about them, they'd feed them Cream of Wheat.

One Saturday Momma and Daddy came back from buying the week's groceries. Besides the heavenly muffins that Daddy always brought from the Henke and Pillot bakery, they had a special treat.

"Cream of Wheat! A box of Cream of Wheat!" Annie and Neecie were ecstatic.

3

Danger Lurks

The house was spic and span clean. The trees, fence, and rocks were all painted. The flowering bushes were neatly trimmed, the rose and flower gardens cleaned and freshened up. Except for last minute touches, the clothes stood ready.

Now came the time for Momma to turn her attention to baking. "You young-uns sit down here on the front porch and shell these pecans for me!" Momma bustled about the kitchen getting all the pans and utensils ready.

Annie, Pelton, Neecie, and Royce sat in a circle smashing pecans, shelling them, and putting the kernels in a bowl for Momma's delicious pecan pies. "By the time I finish cracking these pecans I'm gonna be toothless!"

Annie declared, tossing a handful of pecan kernels into her mouth.

"If you'd use the tack hammer like Momma
said, you wouldn't end up toothless. And quit
eating up the pecans. I swear, you're getting as
greedy as Neecie!" Pelton said. The children
loved to imitate Uncle Porter's words. "I swear"
and "I declare" were two of their favorite expressions to use, but only behind Momma's
back.

"You'd better quit saying them hard words
like, 'I swear,' Pelton, or the Devil's gonna get
you. That's what Momma said happens to folks
that talk ugly," Neecie warned.

After the pecan shelling, the children
picked berries from down the hill for the berry
cobblers. Then they gathered green beans,
cucumbers, tomatoes, and onions from the garden for the side dishes. They went out to the
barn to cull the potatoes Daddy stored there
during the summer months. They selected the
small, sweet red ones for Momma's scrump-
tious potato salad.

As the day wore down the children's voices
filled the summer air across the yard, like
falling leaves against the setting sun.

"This is the best summer we ever had.
Every day is like a holiday!"

"We've done a lot of work."

"Momma's happy 'cause everything looks

so pretty, and that's all I care about," declared Neecie. Her faced glowed with the satisfaction that only comes from hard work.

"I'll say amen to that!"

"Me too!"

"Daddy's happy too!" exclaimed Annie, not wanting to be outdone by Neecie.

Early the next morning Momma sent Annie and Neecie out to the henhouse to gather eggs for lemon pies, strawberry shortcakes, hot rolls, and potato salad. Neecie went rushing into the henhouse ahead of Annie. But right away she came stumbling out and bumped Annie so hard that she almost fell over. "*O-o-o-o-h,* no! Lord have mercy!" she cried softly, almost whispering. She was trembling all over.

"What in the world is wrong with you?" Annie felt her sister's fear. She was anxious to collect the eggs because she didn't like going into the henhouse.

"Snake ... Snake ... Snake ..." Neecie's lips trembled and she could barely get out the words. Her whole body felt cold and weak.

"Oh, dear Lord!" Annie whispered. She looked up and saw an immense chicken snake slithering with powerful coils toward Momma's setting hen. The bird sat quaking with fear, bravely guarding a dozen eggs near to hatching.

"Get Momma. Run! Quick! Get Momma!" Annie nudged Neecie. "I'll stay here and keep

an eye on him!" The children were scared to death of snakes. The minute they saw one they were supposed to run and tell an older head.

Neecie ran screaming, "MOMMA! SNAKE!" She shouted until she saw Momma jump out the door, Daddy's Winchester in her hand. The children always said that Momma must have eyes in the back of her head. She never missed anything.

For just such emergencies, Daddy kept a loaded rifle in the corner of the bedroom. No child was to enter without prior permission. And under *no* circumstances was anyone to touch Daddy's guns, either loaded or unloaded.

The snake slithered closer and closer to the setting hen. The girls could see the long and deadly fangs. The poor bird's eyes bulged and its feathers shook. Momma cooly aimed the rifle. She squeezed the trigger. BANG! The head of the serpent exploded into smithereens. Momma calmly put the gun down against the henhouse door and went over to unruffle the mother hen's feathers.

Pelton and Royce came running up to see what the commotion was about. Pelton reached out to stroke the barrel of the still smoking gun.

"Don't you dare! And don't you ever let me catch you even getting near your Daddy's guns! Guns are for killing. That's their purpose. To kill. See that dead snake? A mistake with a gun and it could be one of you children!"

"I didn't mean no harm," Pelton whispered, his head hanging down almost to his chest. The children never liked to disappoint Momma.

"Yes! You meant harm! The minute you reach for a gun, you're reaching for harm. That's the sole purpose for a gun. Harm! Killing! Yes, your Daddy uses guns to kill animals, to put meat on the table, but he KILLS the animals. Y'all understand? Do you? Guns are used to KILL!"

The children had never heard such a harsh tone from Momma before. It scared them. "We ain't never—ever—gonna touch no gun!" they solemnly declared.

Momma sent them out to read their comic books while she collected the eggs. Then she carried the gun back to her and Daddy's room, and made a mental note to tell him about the snake and gun episode.

4

Time to Get Ready

Juneteenth eve, the day before the Emancipation Proclamation arrived in Galveston. The whole family raced about in a frenzy putting the finishing touches on the preparations.

"You young-uns shake a leg now!"

"Get a move on, Annie! Time and tide wait for no one!"

Momma kept the children moving at a fast clip all that day. There were still quite a number of chores to be done. The ice cream freezer had to be cleaned and readied to crank out the frozen delight. And what a treat it was—soft as air and sweet as honey! Plenty of wood had to be cut, for both the big old wood-burning stove in the kitchen and for the barbecue pit under the lofty oak trees.

Earlier that evening, after he got off work, Daddy had gone to the packing house in Houston to buy sausages, slabs of pork ribs, chickens, and beef short ribs. He had already dickered with a neighbor to buy the lamb, which he called mutton. The meat was stored in the ice-box so it would stay fresh.

As soon as he got home, Daddy busied himself preparing for the celebration. The barbecue pit had to be dug exactly the right size with a lip wide enough for the shovel to be stuck in, so that the burning logs could be stacked just right. That way the fire would be even and could cook the lip-licking barbecue without burning it. "It's the first step to getting the meat cooked like we want it!" Daddy said as he rushed about. He and the older boys dug the big hole in the ground, under the great old oak trees down by the barn, and covered it with chicken wire.

That evening Daddy gave out instructions even during supper, stopping only to eat a quick bite. "Soon's we get through with supper, I'm gonna cut the meat up and ice it down, after your Momma gets through seasoning it. E.P., you run to the store and get a couple of fifty-pound blocks of ice. We need to ice the meat down, cool the soda water, and make the ice cream and polly-pop."

Daddy had been going lickety-split since he

had gotten home from work. He had been pushing himself so hard because it was a labor of love. Family members from far and near would be at the small Southeast Texas farm, nestled down amidst the great tall pines, oaks, and elms. They were coming to celebrate family and freedom.

Daddy wanted everything to be just right for the entire family. He wanted the celebration to be the equal of the solemn yet joyful parties Grandpa Harrison and Grandma Anne had always had when he was growing up on the same little farm. They were ex-slaves, and that gave their festivities extra special meaning. Daddy wanted to be sure that feeling was never lost.

Finally, after supper, after the chores, after the washing up, Daddy, Momma, Uncle Porter, and Aunt Alice sat on the front porch with the children to catch their breath.

"Whew! I mean to tell you, we truly put in one long hard day today, didn't we, Daddy?" Neecie gave a tired little sigh and cozied up to Daddy. She was small for her age and too tiny to do any serious work. What she had done was wear herself out, running around, getting in everybody's way, occasionally toting and fetching.

"I'll say amen to that!" Royce mimicked Uncle Porter. Royce was the youngest in the family and entirely too small to do much work at all. He and Neecie were the fetchers and toters for the bigger family members. "Yes indeed!

I'll sure say amen to that!" He nuzzled up to Daddy too.

"Did you hear them two, Pelton? Did you hear 'em? I tell you they truly take the cake, don't they? Why, we're the ones done all the work! Done worked our fingers plumb to the bone. All they did was run around getting in the way! Now they sit 'round here claiming to be tired. Huh! That beats anything I ever heard before!" Annie declared with indignation. She wanted some credit for all the work that she and Pelton had done helping the grown-ups get everything ready. She probably wanted a little attention too. She kept casting an envious eye at Neecie and Royce over there, cozying up to Daddy.

"Shoots! I'm too tired. Don't make me no never mind what they say, we know who done the work," Pelton sighed, then propped his slender sun-baked brown frame up against a pillar of the porch. He squirmed about until he was comfortable. "Get away from me!" he shouted, as he swatted a pesky mosquito. "Huh! They can say whatsoever they got a mind to!"

"Now, now! Don't you young-uns start squabbling like a bunch of old wet hens! This is a happy time. A time for family and friends to celebrate and enjoy life together." Uncle Porter said, and sternly shook a stubby finger at the four rambunctious children.

"*Aw-w-w*, don't pay 'em no mind. They're all right, just all up in the air and excited 'bout them big doin's tomorrow," Daddy declared, bracing his thin, tired frame against a white porch pillar. He gave five-year-old Royce and seven-year-old Neecie a tight hug.

Annie looked over at Daddy hugging Neecie and Royce. "Humph!" she muttered as she sidled over closer to Daddy.

"Why don't you tell 'em one of your stories Porter? That'll settle 'em down. They all say you're the finest storyteller 'round these parts!" Aunt Alice's tiny, high-pitched voice commanded respect as she rocked back and forth in Momma's rocking chair.

"Yeah, Porter, tell 'em a story 'bout the slavery times. That'll set the tone for tomorrow's big doin's. Let 'em know why we're celebrating," Daddy added, as he reached over and gave one of Annie's skinny brown pigtails a playful tug.

"Yeah, Uncle Porter, tell us about the slavery times!" Annie smiled happily as Daddy gave her a pat on the head.

Uncle Porter paused dramatically, swatted a mosquito with his gnarled hand and looked slyly from face to face. "Which one of them there slaveries would y'all be talking 'bout? I'd sure like to know!"

Pelton, who remembered all of the family

stories almost word for word, jumped to his feet. "Y'all hear that?" He looked around at his family sitting contentedly on the porch. The evening breeze of summer fluttered the oaks and elms and made the cornfields whisper. "He's playing with us again! Uncle Porter's playing with us! Everybody knows it wasn't but one slavery!"

"Well, I swear! Wasn't but one slavery! Ha!" Uncle Porter mimicked Pelton and scoffed at him at the same time. "You see here, y'all didn't learn nothing in that Sunday school class Sister Augusta taught last Sunday. She told y'all 'bout one of them there other slaveries." Uncle Porter shook his round head with the balding spot on top. "Don't y'all remember? Think! You got to think! Learn to use your heads for more than a hat rack!"

Neecie jumped to her feet, shouting "YES! YES! I remember! I remember! IT WAS ISRA-EL'S KIDS! We learned all about Israel's kids! That old mean lowdown Fay-row had 'em in bonnets!" Neecie gleefully swung her hips, clapped her hands, and smiled broadly. She was so excited to have been the first to remember the other slavery.

The grown-ups fell out laughing. "Israel's kids! Heh, heh, heh! Had 'em in bonnets! Ha, ha, ha!" Finally, Momma, wiping tears from her eyes with the back of her work worn hand, said, "Neecie, sweetie, you got the right idea! It was the children of Israel Old Pharaoh was holding in bondage. Go on and tell 'em 'bout it Mr. Porter. They need to know that we're not the only ones ever held in slavery, but we sure were the last! And I know we praise the good Lord for that!"

"AMEN!" everybody said.

Before Uncle Porter could say a word, Royce, who had sat quietly taking it in, jumped to his feet. "Bond-age? That's a new word. I don't understand that word, Momma. What's a bond-age?"

All of the children loved to read. They especially loved for Momma to read to them, but Royce was the most inquisitive. He always wanted to know what the new words meant, and was forever using them in conversation.

"It's just another word for slavery. Shoots, it's all right there in the Bible. Y'all keep on going to Sunday school, you're gonna learn all about Moses and the children of Israel and old Pharaoh, and how the good Lord made a way for 'em to find their way across the sea and dessert into the promised land." Uncle Porter began to warm to his story.

Suddenly, Annie jumped down off the front porch, pigtails bouncing up and down. "WE KNOW THAT! WE KNOW THAT! Don't we, Neecie?"

"YES! YES!" Neecie shouted, clapping her hands and jumping off the front porch too. "We learned all 'bout that in Sunday school!" She rushed over to where Annie was standing. When Neecie got excited, her long, thick black braids rolled around on her back, like fat chunks of rope blowing hither and thither in a windstorm.

Annie and Neecie joined hands and started hopping and skipping and singing out the ancient spiritual they had learned in Sunday school. Screeching in their loudest and most piercing voices, the sisters put heart and soul into the music.

When Israel was in Egypt land,
LET MY PEOPLE GO!
They cried so hard they could not stand,
LET MY PEOPLE GO!
Go down Moses, way down in Egypt land,
LET MY PEOPLE GO!
And tell old Pharaoh, I said,
LET MY PEOPLE GO!

"We knew it! We knew it!" Neecie clapped her hands excitedly.

"We just didn't know it was about slavery and all. Now we done learned something else for our memory bank that Momma told us about." Breathing hard, Annie plopped back down on the front porch beside Momma.

"Well, now, y'all can thank your Uncle Porter for teaching you 'bout it. Y'all know how I truly believe that the more we can learn 'bout other people's trials and tribulations, the more we'll all be able to 'preciate what we've got, no matter how humble it may seem." Despite their struggles, everyone knew in their hearts what Momma said was true.

The little circle of family fell quiet, each one reflecting on his or her memories. After a while Daddy said, "I suspect that it's time you young-uns got ready for bed. Tomorrow's not only a busy day, it's gonna be a long day. Our Ma and Pa always taught us that you need a good night's sleep, when a big day like tomorrow is coming at you. Didn't they, Brother Porter?"

Uncle Porter opened his mouth to answer Daddy. Before he could get a word out, the children moaned in one voice, throwing back their heads and rolling their eyes in dismay. *"O-o-o-o-h-h-h! No! No! No!"*

"We can't go to bed now," Royce declared. "Why, we haven't heard 'bout our bond-age yet." He looked around proudly, hoping that everyone had noticed his use of the new word.

"Y'all can hear 'bout our bondage tomorrow night." Momma smiled in spite of herself. She took pride in helping the children learn new vocabulary and good speaking skills. Her deep brown eyes sparkled with happiness at what her children were learning.

"NO! NO! NO!" They chorused in one voice.

"You always make us go to bed, just when the story gets to be most inter-resting!" Annie hoped to get on Momma's good side by using vocabulary from a story Momma had read to them.

"Yeah, you always make us go to bed, just when things get to be inter-resting!"

"Will you promise not to make us go to bed tomorrow night?"

The whining and begging continued until Momma hushed them with her powerful gaze. "I promise. Tomorrow is a special day. Y'all can stay up just as late as you can keep your eyes open."

"Well, now, Momma's done promised. Everybody heard, and we all know how you and Daddy done taught us that your word is your bond. So tomorrow we get to stay up as long as we can and learn all 'bout our people's bond-age." Pelton looked slyly out of the corner of his deep mysterious eyes, to make sure everybody noticed his use of the new word as well.

Annie, Pelton, Neecie, and Royce headed sleepily into the house to get ready for bed. It had been a long day, and they could barely keep their eyes open. "I'm kind of glad Momma made us go to bed. I'm so tired, my legs can't hardly carry me in the house," Neecie whispered when she was out of earshot of the older heads. She yawned sleepily.

"One of you young men come run your Uncle Porter and Aunt Alice home," Daddy called out. "It done got too late for 'em to try 'n walk home."

"Here I come, Daddy, I'll take 'em." E. P., one of the older boys who had been snoozing in the cool breezes of the upstairs deck, volunteered to drive Uncle Porter and Aunt Alice home. It hadn't been long since he had bought his pre-owned green Chevy. He loved showing off as he cruised through the small town flirting with the pretty girls. As he drove by, the young women pretended to swoon and coyly called out his name. E. P. thought himself very handsome.

5

The Big Day Arrives

Early the next morning, June 19, Daddy was up at the crack of dawn. He and the older boys got the fire started in the freshly dug barbecue pit.

"Boys, I'm going out to the field to pull the corn. The fresher it is when you cook it, the better the flavor is. Y'all keep a sharp eye on the fire. Soon as it's ready we want to get the meat on!" He called out over his shoulder as he departed into the corn field. He carried a fifty-pound tow sack in which the cow and horse feed had come. His hands flew from ear to ear, each one bursting with sweet gold and white kernels. Soon, he had stuffed the tow sack full of the field's bounty.

"Looks like we're gonna make a fine crop o'

corn this harvest," Daddy observed to himself
as he carried the bulging sack back to the
house. He put it down by the back porch, for
the children to shuck, clean the silks off, and
wash. Then he built a fire under Momma's big
iron wash pot that she boiled the white clothes
and bed linens in, and filled it with water to
boil the corn.

It wasn't too long before the rest of the family started stirring on the little farm. Everybody's clean clothes had been starched, ironed,
and laid out for later in the morning. The family would get cleaned up and dressed before the
relatives came. There was still plenty of work
to do before they could get all decked out in
their special Juneteenth clothes.

"Look, Neecie! We prayed for a beautiful
Juneteenth, and God's done sent us a marvel!"
said Annie, as she and Neecie peeked anxiously
out of the bedroom window. The sun burst
forth in a cloudless blue sky. A cool breeze
blowing in from the Gulf of Mexico made the
starched ruffles on the white Priscilla curtains
sway back and forth. In the warm weather
throughout the year, the family kept the windows open both day and night. There was no
crime in the town. It was a close community
where everybody knew people's comings and
goings. Air-conditioning was unheard of in the

small towns and hamlets that dotted the Texas landscape.

"It's going to be a wonderful Juneteenth, Annie! I'm so excited I'm 'bout to bust!" Neecie clapped her hands as she fell back on the bed.

"Come on, Neecie! We got to get in the kitchen and help Momma. There's still a whole lots to be done." The awesome fun-filled day ahead made the girl's hearts pound with excitement.

"It's time to get the meat on the coals, boys. Shake a leg!" It was around six-thirty that morning when E. P. echoed Daddy, "The fire's just right for cooking now, y'all. Let's get that meat out here so we can put it on the pit! TIME'S A WASTIN'!" Their shouts stirred Pelton and Royce. They grabbed a tub heavy with meat and lugged it out to the pit. Annie and Neecie grabbed the other wash tub. Momma had seasoned the sides of beef, sides of ribs, mutton, chickens, and other meat for the barbecue and iced it down the night before in the tin tubs.

"Whew! These old tubs are sure heavy!"

"Yeah, they must weigh a ton!"

The four children continued to complain as they went wagging and dragging the tubs along.

Daddy arranged the meat on the pit, in his special cooking order. The fragrant clouds began to ascend to heaven. The meat slowly sizzled, the flavors of smoke and spice blending and mingling. The whole farm had the rich smoke wafting over it. Daddy mopped the barbecue with his special recipe (which was mostly oil, vinegar, lemons, garlic, and onions). And when the fragrance mingled with the aroma of freshly shucked boiling corn, bubbling madly in the old iron pot, everybody's mouth started watering.

Pretty soon Uncle Porter came trudging purposefully down the road. His arthritic legs struggled to hold up his round body after the long walk. He clutched a brown paper sack under his arm. "My nose told me it was time to get on down here," he said, rubbing his hands together. Aunt Alice would be coming down later when the rest of the family started to congregate.

"Come help us turn the ice cream freezer, Uncle Porter!" Annie shouted to the round little man. Annie, almost nine, was getting good at ice cream making.

Neecie peeled the boiled potatoes and eggs for the salad, and Momma chopped them up into dainty little cubes. Then she cut up the green onions, pickles, and olives. Momma saw Uncle Porter sit down on the porch. "Come on in, Mr. Porter. The more hands, the faster the work."

"Heh, heh, heh!" Uncle Porter didn't much believe in working hard and getting himself all flustered. Winded from the three-mile walk from his house to the farm, he had sat down on the steps for a moment. "Where's the sodawater? I brought a dozen or so bottles to add to the pot."

He got up and put the sack of bottles down in the tub of ice with the rest of the strawberry sodas. Then he went out under the trees where the men were sopping and turning the savory barbecue. Uncle Porter knew it was time to start sampling the meat.

"Let me taste!"

"Let me!"

"I wanna taste too!"

"Give me a rib!"

"Yummy! Y'all outdone yourselves this time!"

No one had stopped for much of anything to eat on this vey special day, so everybody stood around "sampling" the juicy, lip-licking good barbecue. Momma sent out a loaf of bread and a gallon bucket of ice cold punch that the children called "so-good," and the celebrating started.

"Young-uns, come on and pack this ice cream down now, then get washed up and put on your clean clothes. It won't be too long now before the rest of the family's gonna start gathering!" Momma bustled the children off to their tasks.

Daddy, the older boys, Pelton (who was already ten), and Royce went down to Old Rickett's gully for a quick swim. They wanted to cool off and wash the smoke away. Uncle

Porter stayed behind tending to the barbecue. He mopped the meat, making sure each cut was thickly coated. He turned it with home-made forks that Daddy had made. Two days before, he had walked in the woods looking for saplings or branches with a natural fork to them. After he had found several, he cut them to use for the cooking.

Momma and the girls washed up and changed clothes at the house. Annie and Neecie put fresh ribbons on their pigtails. They matched their yellow socks with their yellow, flowered ruffled dresses. Even though they knew their outfits had been flour sacks just days before, they couldn't believe when they looked in the mirror. They were that elegant. "Momma said that we could wear our good patent leather Sunday shoes," Neecie said as she preened before the glass.

"Yeah, but remember, she told us that we couldn't go running and playing after we got through eating our Juneteenth meal, if we kept our good shoes on!"

"So? We'll just pull 'em off! It's how we look when everybody gets here that counts any-way!" Neecie shot back.

Annie and Neecie were prancing back and forth in front of the mirror, admiring them-selves, when they heard the blowing horns. Cars, flatbed trucks, pick-up trucks, and even a bicycle came streaming down the road toward the house. "Here they come! *O-h-h-h-h*!! Here they come!" Neecie shouted as she and Annie sprinted out of the house.

The caravan was loaded with relatives and friends. Some hung out the windows, others rode on the runningboards. Every seat was taken and quite a few laps too. The vehicles streamed down the road lined with the white-washed pines, oaks, and elms. That simple but stately path led to the little Texas farm with the story and a half house, surrounded by gleaming white pickets. As they came into view, with horns honking happily, everybody started singing.

> *Hail! Hail! The gang's all here!*
> *What the heck do we care!*
> *What the heck do we care!*
> *Hail! Hail! The gang's all here!*
> *What the heck do we care now?*

The singing and the shouting resounded in the summer sunlight as the cars and trucks stopped under the great old oaks. Cousins, aunts, uncles, and friends piled out. Momma and Poppa came as fast as their old legs could carry them. Daddy's brothers and sisters ran out to greet the family. All had come to the great eightieth June-teenth Freedom Celebration! Hallelujah!

Everyone had brought something. There

were at least a hundred brown bags filled with sodas and candy. Every woman seemed to have a loaf of home baked bread with her. And more kinds of cakes and pies than the children could even imagine!

The greeting and the hugging and the kissing began.

"Look how big this child has gotten!"

"My goodness! These children are growing like weeds!"

"Come here and give your auntie a kiss!"

The aunts, uncles, cousins, and grandparents adored each child over and over. Then the hugging and kissing went all around again and again until the eyes of the adults filled with tears. Finally, Daddy said, "All right now! That's enough of all this carrying on! We got loads of great food here. So let's get this show on the road, y'all. It's time to eat!"

Daddy, Uncle Porter, and the other men put long planks of wood on the sawhorses to make the tables to hold that immense feast. Momma and the other women put clean, white sheets on for tablecloths. "Here, Annie, you children spread these blankets out under them shade trees for you young-uns to sit on. Pelton, you and Royce and these other children, take the chairs from the kitchen and dining room. Then grab those benches and the rocking chair from the front porch. We're gonna need 'em for the

older heads to sit down on." Momma seemed to be everywhere as she bustled about, giving directions and getting ready to feed the big gathering of kinfolk, friends, and family.

"Here we come, y'all!" Grandma called out. All the women began bringing out platter after platter and bowl after bowl of delectable delights from the kitchen. Daddy had put most of the barbecued meat in the clean tubs, but even the Christmas turkey platter ran over with the delicious barbecue.

The makeshift table sagged in the middle, being so loaded down with the feast. And what a cornucopia it was! People could scarcely believe there was that much food in all of Texas! From Momma's garden there were sliced tomatoes, crisp cucumbers, leafy green salads, shiny beans, beets, and pickled peppers. Huge bowls of potato salad dotted the table. Every three feet was a large tray of corn from Daddy's fields. And next to those were bowls of Momma's special baked beans that had been cooking in the wood burning stove for the better of two days. One whole end of a table was left for dessert. The pies and cakes delighted the eye and whetted the appetite.

"Just look at that table . . . Uh . . . Uh . . . Uh!" one of the cousins gasped.

"I ain't never seen that much food before in my life!" said another.

"Come on, y'all, let's gather 'round the table and hold hands. Let's thank the good Lord for our freedom, for all this wonderful food, and all the other blessings he's done be-stowed on us." Daddy solemnly intoned the blessing. The words moved the hearts of everyone there and they joined in as one voice, one soul.

"Gracious Lord, make us truly
grateful for the
food we're about to receive.
Thank you for the
fruits of the earth in their season
and the labors of those who harvest them.
Give us nourishment for our bodies
and our spirit,
for Christ the Redeemer's sake,
Amen."

"Well, come on, y'all, let's eat!" Daddy led the line of grown-ups and children around the table with their plates and forks. The family members and friends made a big to-do over the wonderful eats.

"I tell you, Eddie, you sure outdone yourself on the barbecue this year!"

"My! My! This mutton is as tender as a mother's love!"

"Suwillow, I don't believe there's a soul on the face of the earth that can best your potato salad!"

There was plenty of iced tea, "so-good," and sodawater for drinking, and ice-cold watermelon and ice cream for later on. The feast lasted until late in the afternoon. Everyone had eaten more than they had thought they could.

"Let's take the dishes into the house and wash 'em, y'all. Then we can go play," said Annie. The girls took the dishes into the house to wash them. Royce, Pelton, and the boys picked up the throwaway things and put them in a tow sack. Then they collected all of the edible food scraps and put them in a slop bucket for the hogs. They put the bones and meat scraps in a brown paper bag to save for the dogs. On a farm, there's hardly anything to throw away with so many mouths to feed. The rest of the food was left on the tables covered over with clean sheets. Anyone could go back for thirds or fourths.

Those who didn't have to help in the cleanup, or had finished their job, sat under the trees swapping tales. They talked about survival, living in the city, and the family history. They told heartfelt stories about loved ones who had long ago gone on to their reward. And they told funny stories about each other as well.

Celebration and Remembrance

"We've done cleaned up the kitchen, Momma. Can we go play?" Royce's quiet voice reflected the hopes of all the children.

"Yes, but don't you young-uns go far from the house," Momma warned.

Annie, Neecie, Pelton, Royce, the cousins, the friends—all went flying around the corner of the house, out into the back yard to play hide-and-go-seek. "Y'all go on and hide! I'll come searching for you when everybody's done hid. Y'all holler MAY HIE! when I ask if you're ready."

Neecie always liked to be first when it was time to play. She leaned on the big pecan tree, resting her head on her folded arms. She was supposed to close her eyes, but Neecie liked to peek a little to see where the other children were hiding. Finally, she called out, "BUSHEL

OF WHEAT! BUSHEL OF RYE! EVERYBODY READY HOLLER MAY HIE!"

"MAY HIE!" a hiding child called from behind the smokehouse.

"MAY HIE!" Another called from behind the henhouse.

"MAY HIE!" called a child from under the house.

"READY OR NOT, HERE I COME!" And Neecie tore out running. The city cousins and friends loved playing at the farm. Most of them lived in apartments, where there wasn't much room for playing.

Time passed quickly. The children enjoyed their games. The grown-ups caught up on all the family news, good and bad. Soon the twilight sun disappeared and the evening sky began to deepen.

"You young-uns come and get your ice cream and cake. It's getting pretty dark, so it's 'bout time to be getting on the road. Your folks gonna have to start back pretty soon so they're not on the road at all hours!" The playing children heard Momma and raced back to the picnic area. Heaping bowls of ice cream and delicious chunks of cake greeted them. There was more *oohing* and *aahing* over the desserts. "I guess it's 'bout time for us to get started back," Grandma said, bustling about gathering up things.

"But we just got here!"

"Can we spend the night?"

"I'm not ready!" the cousins chorused.

The family members divided up the left-overs to take home with them, as the ice-box at the farm wasn't big enough to hold them all. Then the cars and trucks, loaded down with happy people, started winding up the road, back to homes in the city, or the little town down the way.

"Bye y'all."

"See ya next time."

"Come see us, ya hear?"

"Bye."

"Bye-bye."

They shouted goodbyes and farewells long after both guest and host knew the other was out of earshot. When only the sound of hoot-owls and the night wind played across the farm, the older boys got dressed up to go into the little town nearby. The citizens had built a big platform down by the schoolhouse. They hired a band from the city for the occasion. The young men wanted to do some dancing with the pretty girls.

Momma went in to put away the last few dishes. Daddy, Uncle Porter, and Aunt Alice sat on the front porch. Royce plopped his head on Daddy's knee, saying, "I'm plumb worn out!" The other children built a smoke pot to chase away the mosquitos. Everyone sat quietly in the cool June evening. They left all the chairs out under the trees, except for the good ones from the dining-room.

"Uncle Porter? Tell us the story again 'bout our ant-cestors and 'bout how come we always celebrate Juneteenth every year. You told us last night that you'd tell us 'bout 'em." Neecie's eyes were soft brown pools of hope that gave a special light in the darkness.

"And 'bout the bon-dage too," Royce added sleepily.

"Not ant-cestors, Neecie." Momma smiled as she joined them on the porch. "*An*-cestors . . . that means our family who lived before we did."

"Neecie's done gone and got it wrong again," observed Pelton dryly, while jiggling the moss around in the smoke pot.

"Yes, Uncle Porter, tell us again 'bout how Harriet Tubman and them others put all of those slaves on that big old train and drove 'em up North to freedom," said Annie.

"Yeah, that big old train what drove up under the ground!" Neecie chimed in.

"It wasn't no train, no such," Pelton pointed out, squinting his pale brown eyes to keep away the smoke.

"Daddy told me and Royce that it wasn't no railroad at all. It was a bunch of secret hiding places and such where they hid them runaway slaves so they wouldn't get caught! They say sometimes it was in Christian people's attics, basements, or even smokehouses. Other times they hid in the water amongst the snakes and alligators. That way them low down slave-catchers' mean old dogs wouldn't get a whiff of 'em. That's what it was." As if to emphasize his point, Pelton sat down with authority as he finished speaking.

"Pelton's right. I 'member when Daddy said it," Royce added quietly.

"Well, I don't care what it was, long as it got them poor slaves out of that mess!" Annie snapped huffily.

"Now we can celebrate the whole thing every Juneteenth with lots of good food. Barbecue and ice cream and so-good and everything! Why, it's better than a birthday party!" Neecie patted her full tummy and thought about her own birthday in a few months.

"For goodness' sakes, Neecie! You're forever thinking 'bout your stomach! You're the greediest person on the face of the earth!" Annie glared at her sister. It galled her that Pelton and Royce knew more about the people who had helped the slaves to freedom than she did. She made a mental note to read about the underground railroad and Harriet Tubman.

Aunt Alice, who was rocking gently in Momma's rocker, paused. "You young-uns stop that squabbling! You hear? You're acting like a bunch of old setting hens. I do declare, Eddie, y'all letting them young-uns grow up like weeds!! Squabbling and carrying on! Uh-uh-uh!

Like weeds! They'll come to no good end, mark my word."

"You young-uns be still now," Daddy gently warned. "Let your Uncle Porter tell you 'bout the freedom. He's the best storyteller in the family."

"And that's another thing!" Aunt Alice snarled. "I done rethought this slave story telling, and I'm sick and tired of hearing them old depressing stories 'bout slavery times. You're gonna fool 'round here and give them young-uns nightmares! I think it's silly to keep reminding us 'bout all that negative slavery stuff! It's over and done with now. We ought to forget about it and get on with our lives. Celebrating is one thing, sad old depressing stories is another. Let's just forget about it!"

"THE TRUTH IS THE LIGHT!" Uncle Porter declared, jumping up and waving his pudgy fist in the air. "If we forget 'bout slavery time, what's gonna keep it from happening again? Huh? Just tell me that!"

"I'll say A-MEN to that! And the truth ain't never hurt nobody, as far as I can tell," Daddy declared righteously.

"Yes, Uncle Porter, tell us 'bout our history," Pelton pleaded.

"Well, well, y'all know how they brought the people over here from Africa a long time ago to work the fields. They called it the African slave trade. Sometimes they'd catch 'em while the young fellows went out hunting. Other

times their own people sold 'em off like livestock. Then the slavers packed 'em into them
big old boats, packed 'em just like sardines!
Most times there wasn't even enough room for
'em to turn over. They would have to just lay in
one spot, chained down, for days on end.

"Hundreds and thousands and millions
died. Millions more got so sick they were never
the same. No telling exactly how many died,
'cause there ain't no good records. They wasn't
no more than cows or pigs dying, so they just
threw 'em overboard into the sea! That's how
they brought our people over here to sell as
slaves. No different than a cow or horse!"
Uncle Porter's hands shook with anger. He
paused to catch his breath.

"Oh . . . oh . . . oh sweet Jesus," Pelton
mumbled softly, shaking his head.

"Have mercy!" Annie whispered, wiping
her eyes.

"That's a sin and a shame!" Royce said,
using one of Daddy's expressions. He swal-
lowed loudly, to clear up the big lump that was
in his throat.

"Lord! Lord!" Neecie shivered and climbed
into Daddy's arms for protection.

Uncle Porter cleared his throat and paused
dramatically before he continued the story. He
wanted to add an element of suspense and hold
his audience's attention. "That underground
railroad run by Miz Tubman wasn't really

under the ground. Underground is just a word that means secret-like. So's nobody could catch 'em. Anyhow, that fine lady Miz Tubman, and all them good Christian folks helping her, sure gave a hand hiding a mighty heap of them runaway slaves. Otherwise those freedom seekers could never have made it to the North!"

"How in the world did she do that? Wasn't she scared?"

"Well, it was just like I done said, all them fine Christian folks helped her. Both black and white gave that little lady a hand with the escaping slaves." Uncle Porter rubbed his pudgy hands together with evident satisfaction.

Royce's eyes widened. "You mean white folks helped slaves escape?" Despite his age, his face was incredulous.

"Why, Lord, yes!" Uncle Porter answered. "Why, they never could have got that many slaves out to freedom if all kinds of folks hadn't lent a hand."

Daddy nodded thoughtfully. "The color of a body's skin ain't got nothin' to do with whether he's good or evil, or whether he turns a person a favor or not. It ain't what's on the outside that counts. It's what's in a body's heart."

Uncle Porter continued. "And before long, when the War Between the States broke out, the Civil War that is, it was a whole lots easier to make it up North. Plenty of slaves escaped to freedom land and joined the Union Army.

Harriet Tubman even helped out the army whenever she could! And pretty soon ..." Uncle Porter paused dramatically again and looked skyward.

"Whoooppeee! Freedom came, didn't it? And the slaves were set free! And there wasn't no more bon ... bon ... bon-dage!" Neecie exclaimed, clapping her hands.

"Amen, child! I mean to tell you! On January 1, 1863, 'bout two years after the Civil War started, President Lincoln set the slaves free. It was the Emancipation Proclamation! 'Course back then, they didn't have radios and telephones like today. So all the states didn't get the news 'bout the freedom at the same time. The announcement hit Texas in Galveston on June 19, 1865, 'round two and a half years later on.

"Yessir, that was the day when a big old sailin' ship docked at Galveston. The Civil War was just gettin' over. General Granger and the men on that ship were the first ones to tell folks here 'bout that freedom proclamation!"

"And then everybody celebrated and had a good time!"

"And they named it 'Juneteenth'!"

"And that's how come we celebrate and eat plenty of barbecue and cake and drink so-good. 'cause of what our ant-cestors done! Ain't it, Daddy?" The voices of the children rang out in the night.

"That's the beautiful truth!" Daddy declared.

"Mind you, it wasn't no flower bed of ease for them freed slaves," Uncle Porter reminded them. "Ain't no schools to teach a body how to be free men and women. But they had a good time when they heard the news. Heh! Heh! Heh! They say that when some of 'em heard it they shouted and danced and jumped up and down. Others fell on their knees and started to pray. They sang and praised the Lord. They told 'bout how the Lord had delivered 'em from bondage, just like He delivered Moses and the children of Israel from old Pharaoh . . ." Uncle Porter paused at the wonder of it all. His voice became real soft. "Yes sir, just like Moses and the children of Israel . . ."

"That's our song! We learned 'bout that in Sunday school!"

Annie and Neecie jumped up and started to sing again.

Go down Moses, way down in Egypt land,
        LET MY PEOPLE GO!
    And tell old Pharaoh, I said,
        LET MY PEOPLE GO!

They clapped their hands and sang at the tops of their screeching voices.

"Hush up, y'all, I want to hear 'bout the freed men and women," Pelton said. "Go on, Uncle Porter, tell us what happened next."

"There wasn't much money left on the Southern plantations when the Civil War ended. They'd done poured it all into the fight against the North. But whole lots of the freed men and women scraped together enough money and goods to leave the plantations where they'd been slaves. They struck out on their own with their heads held high. Most of 'em headed North. The families were scattering in every direction. Some family members never did see each other no more. Our family was lucky." Uncle Porter shook his head and wiped a tear with the back of his hand.

"I want to hear about my Grandpa Harrison. He's my favorite ancestor," Royce said quietly, looking up at Uncle Porter with his mysterious brown eyes.

"Well, your Grandpa was traveling with the master when he heard 'bout that freedom proclamation. Just like they did here, the people praised the Lord and danced and really carried on. The news hadn't got to Texas yet, but Pa knew it'd get here sooner or later. When Pa was a young slave, he'd stand in them cotton fields in the sizzling sun, lean on his hoe and think, 'The Lord's got to make a way.' It ain't many that done what Pa done.

"Before Pa was born, the master left Louisiana and moved to Texas. There was plenty of land and water, and property was dirt cheap! The master brung our Grandpa Simon, Grandma Eliza, and Uncle Mack with him. Your Grandpa Harrison, his sisters Leatha and Jane, and brothers Frank and Tobe were all born right here in Harris County. The master sold all the children except Mack and Pa to other plantations. Pa never saw Aunt Leatha again . . .

"Ma came from Virginia. We don't know how she got here, but the word was Pa brought 'er. He was always traveling hither and yon with the master on business trips. So we just always figured his work took him to Virginia where he got Ma. She lived in slavery and worked up at the big house, but she had her freedom papers. She come here free!

"When freedom came for everyone, Pa was 'bout fifteen and Ma 'bout eleven. Least that's what those census papers say. Pa started thinking on where him, Ma, Grandma, Grandpa, and Uncle Mack would settle down. He wasn't 'bout to leave Harris County or even Texas. All his contacts he'd done made, travelling 'round with the master, would come into good play now. Pa wanted to buy land and own businesses, just like white folk. He'd done helped the master run the business since he was no more 'n seven or eight years old. He wanted to be where there'd be plenty of water for the crops and all. Pa saved his money, burying it in a safe place. He worked hard, cutting and selling wood, catching, taming, and selling wild horses, and doing other odd jobs, and squirreled away his money and made his plans.

"Ma had lived in the 'Big House' since they

had brung her here from Virginia. She done fancy sewing for them fine dressing ladies, and they paid her. She and Pa always knew they'd get married, and they done it right. Ma was not the type of woman to hear tell of 'taking up' or broom jumping. They went through a big riga-marole for the marrying: to the county judge, up to the county courthouse, then to the church house for the marrying, then on to the eating and celebrating. Ma wanted a proper wedding, and she got it: white frilly dress and veil and the works. Why, folks far and near still talk 'bout her highfalutin' Virginia ways.

"'Course, it wasn't all that simple and easy, 'cause not only did they have to work hard to save enough cash, they had to keep a sharp eye out all the time for them trashy paddy-rollers." Uncle Porter's eyes grew steely in the moon-light just thinking about it.

"PADDY-ROLLERS!" the children cried.

"You've never mentioned nothing 'bout no paddy-rollers before, Uncle Porter. I believe you done stretched the truth again!" Annie declared, giving Uncle Porter a stern eye and a broad smile.

"Nope! I'd done forgot all 'bout them evil people 'till me and your Pa talked 'bout Grand-ma Annie's stories the other night. He re-minded me 'bout 'em. A bunch of freed slaves turned bad used to hide out and waylay the freed slaves. The varmits stole what little goods and money the freed people had worked so hard for. Sometimes they'd kill 'em. It was hard times for the freed slaves, mighty hard. The good Lord sure looked out for our kin folk. Pa and the rest of our kin survived those hard times. Amen." The moon revealed a thoughtful expression all around the circle as they listened to Uncle Porter's words.

"It was not too long after the first Juneteenth that your Grandpa Harrison started buying land, and the other kin started to congregate. And that's how we happen to be on this very farm," Daddy said.

"Pretty soon, Pa lit out to find his sold-off family. He never found his sis Leatha, but he found Aunt Jane, Uncle Tobe, Uncle Frank, and their families. Some said Aunt Leatha had been resold to a Louisiana slaveholder.

"Ma's folks come from Virginia, and 'till this day that side of the family is a mystery. Poor Ma had no mother or father . . . nobody. Just Pa and us. Slavery done that to Ma. Stole her family." Uncle Porter would shed a tear when he reached the slavery and Ku Klux Klan parts of the family history.

"But Ma and Pa and our kinfolks had the first family Juneteenth celebration right here on this land on June 19, 1866. They say it was a very special time. Plenty to eat! Plenty to drink! Dancing and everything!" Uncle Porter exclaimed.

A happy silence fell over the porch and the only sounds to be heard were the chirping of crickets and the rustling of trees in the soft June evening. Suddenly, the sound of music came bouncing through the trees and down the road from the Silver Dollar Night Club, flowing over the Juneteenth celebrators.

"Speaking of dancing, you hear that music, Uncle Porter?" Pelton jumped to his feet, popped his fingers, and started cutting a jig.

"I know good and well you ain't fixing to get up and start dancing with them young-uns, old man!" Aunt Alice warned Uncle Porter.

"Just watch my feet!" Uncle Porter answered, as he swung Neecie through the air.

"Me? Watch your feet? You better watch them old knees of yours that arthur-ritus done crippled up!" retorted Aunt Alice.

"Heh! Heh! I ain't 'bout to let a little thing like arthur-ritus stop me from enjoying life!" Uncle Porter snapped his fingers to the music.

"You just keep on trying to play young, old man, and you're gonna end up with a stroke or a heart attack or something, and leave me a widow!" Aunt Alice warned.

"Whoopee-ee, LOOK AT ME, Y'ALL!" Neecie shouted, her pigtails and dress swooshing out in the air.

"Would you look at that old man and them kids! I do declare, Eddie, y'all lettin' them young-uns grow up just like weeds! Look at 'em. Just flouncin' 'round out there to that old honky-tonk music!" Aunt Alice sniffed.

"This ain't just any old day, Alice. It's the day we got our freedom. I don't want my young-uns to forget what our forebearers went through! It keeps us strong. It's a time to celebrate! Why, I remember when you used to cut a pretty good figure on the dance floor yourself, Alice. Heh . . . heh . . . heh!"

Momma smiled and wiped her eyes. "Our young-uns are gonna be just fine. They're gonna have some peaks, and they're gonna have some valleys. Sometimes their row is gonna be awful hard to hoe, but they're gonna be just fine!"

"My Pa always taught me that you got to bend the twig the way you want it to grow. We're bending our little twigs just fine!" Daddy gave Royce a tight squeeze, then pushed him out with the dancers.

Aunt Alice sighed and smiled, in spite of herself, as she looked out at the celebrants all flouncing and cavorting in the front yard, while the music from the old Silver Dollar Night Club flowed over the dancers.

Straighten up and fly right!
Straighten up and stay right!
Cool down Poppa,
Don't you blow your top . . .

Daddy rose up and went over to Aunt Alice, saying, "Come on Sister Alice, stop being such an old killjoy. Come on here and show these folks how to dance!"

"Now you look-a-here, Eddie . . ." Aunt Alice pulled back her hand.

"Look here my eye! Come on here!" Daddy said, dragging the reluctant Aunt Alice to the front yard and whirling her around.

"Now you cut out this foolishness, Eddie! I do declare, you and that old man of mine are actin' just like them loony children you and Suwillow let grow up like weeds!" Aunt Alice said, digging in her heels.

"Go on, Mrs. Alice, you don't live but once, you might as well try to enjoy yourself!" Momma beamed as she moved over to the rocking chair to get a better view of the dancers.

"Ain't that the beautiful truth!" Uncle Porter said, flinging Neecie around, laughing and popping his fingers, in spite of the pain in his arthritic knees.

"WHOOP-E-E-E!" Neecie shouted gleefully.

All the children were leaping and jumping and popping their fingers. All of the tiredness flowed away as the music enveloped them. Pretty soon Aunt Alice flung herself into the spirit of the dance. She was snapping her fingers, shaking her shoulders, and shouting, "Freedom is wonderful! Enjoying life is wonderful! HONEY HUSH!"

Harrison Barrett: "He Casted a Mighty Long Shadow"

The Author Tells the Story
Behind the Story

Harrison Barrett, my grandfather, triumphed over slavery, segregation, and hard times. He became a businessman and Texas land baron, who had big dreams and a clear vision of what he wanted. Uncle Porter always told us, "Pa was a big man; he done big things; dreamt big dreams and made 'em come true. He casted a mighty long shadow."

Sitting on the front porch on warm summer evenings, Uncle Porter would tell us about grandfather, who was born a slave in Harris County, Texas, around 1851. He was a handsome man, tall and broad-shouldered, with brown eyes, light brown skin, and a shock of reddish brown curls. He bought land when slaves and ex-slaves didn't have the right to their own freedom, let alone land. Freedmen and freedwomen often lived on credit and sweat. Their housing was the "quarters," a collection of shacks and shanties. Grandfather managed to find other accommodations.

Hard times hit the South after the war. The ex-masters had precious little money for themselves and none for their former slaves. "Life wasn't no flower bed of ease for ex-slaves," according to Uncle Porter. "Freedom threw most into a tizzy—not knowing which way to turn, or what to do. There was no celebrating for Pa. He'd saved enough money to start buying land. Old man Reuben White owned land from here to yonder. Pa struck a deal; Pa paid the money down and cut wood to build his Pa and Ma a house. When he and Ma got married, Pa had built his own house. Ex-slaves couldn't own land, but Pa had a deal with the Reuben Whites, and by 1866 he'd bought forty-odd acres."

In 1870 Grandfather Harrison and Grandmother Anne had settled into their home. He put Simon and Eliza, his parents, along with his brothers and sister, in neighboring houses. Our grandparents named their first child Jane.

By now Barrett had acquired more than two hundred acres of the Reuben White survey, about twenty-two miles northeast of downtown Houston on the Texas Independence Trail. He donated land and helped build Barrett's school and the Shiloh Missionary Baptist Church. The Reverend Lemuel Henry Langford was the first pastor. It is one of the oldest black churches in the state. The community was called Barrett's Settlement until the mid-1940s, when the government opened a post office. It then became known as Barrett's Station. Today, The Texas Official Highway Travel Map and The Texas Almanac list the community as Barrett.

Grandfather Harrison built his home on the land closest to Peach Creek, a bubbling gully that emptied into the San Jacinto River. "That's where the womenfolk done their washing, the menfolk done their fishing, the churchfolk done their baptizing, and us young-uns done our swimming," Uncle Porter told us. "That's how Pa 'visioned' it, when he first seen that gully."

Not far from the gully stood a natural spring that gave water to the community. Harrison Barrett had several businesses: a sawmill, a sugar refinery, a syrup plant, and, because of the spring, a whiskey distillery. "The menfolk built the houses. The womenfolk and youngsters planted the wisteria, crepe myrtles, lavenders, rose of sharon, petunias, and zinnias. They also planted plum, pear, and peach trees," Uncle Porter said.

Pretty soon, Grandfather declared that the family ought to celebrate its blessings, and years of Juneteenth celebrations started. "Pa didn't do no lot of celebratin' when the freedom news came. He waited 'till he had his family back, a place to live, and a way to live. Now he had something to crow about, and be thankful for.

Pa's fine Juneteenth celebrations got so famous, the only thing to beat 'em was Christmas."

Harrison Barrett kept on working and buying up the Reuben White survey. By 1889, he was able to start registering his land purchases at the Harris County Courthouse. He registered two hundred acres on January 5, 1889. The second batch of land, about 1,000 acres at fifty cents an acre, was registered on February 25, 1893.

"Right after Pa registered all that land up yonder in the courthouse, is when all the terrible trouble started," Uncle Porter said. "People started to tearing down the fences. The livestock would get out and be all up and down Highway 90. One time the Ku Klux Klan people came to kill Pa. They kept yelling, 'Niggers ain't got no business owning this much land!' A Klan guy with a gun held it to Pa's head, trying to make him sign a deed claiming so much of the land belonged to them. Pa wouldn't do it. He told 'em, 'Y'all gonna have to kill me. I'll die 'fore I let you take land that I worked hard for!' he declared.

"Lord, Lord, the young-uns started crying and begging Pa to please sign the paper. Pa made us kids go to the house. We ran and told Ma. She came flying, didn't stop 'till she got to Pa. 'Put your mark on the paper Harrison,' she told him. 'Go on! Put your mark on it. We can get some more land!'

"That Klan guy hit Pa on the head and told him, 'You better listen to her, boy. That's a smart nigger gal you got there.' Ma locked her arms around Pa's waist, pleading with him to put his mark on the paper. Pa put that X on the paper, and him and Ma came back to the house. Pa sat down on the front porch and held his bleeding head. 'Course Pa knew how to write. Ma made him put that X 'cause she figured that later on down the road, some of us might be able to get the land back. We never did, and now they're building fine houses on the land, and none of 'em can get a clean title."

Things got so bad with fences being torn down and livestock being stolen that Grandfather Harrison started to sell off land. He sold hundred-acre parcels to various white families around Barrett. He rented the land over on the hill, next to old Highway 90, to the old Major.

Grandfather Harrison taught his children the businesses. An early census listed he and Grandmother Anne as having six children. By the 1900 census they had twelve. Grandfather Harrison trained his son Harrison, Jr., to ride and break wild horses. Once they had more than one hundred horses.

"We'd a been rich," Uncle Porter said. "Set for life, except a lowdown white man lied and made like he was from the army. Pa and Harrison broke them horses for the army. That man came, and him and a bunch of other white guys drove them horses off. They told Pa they'd send the check for $500 in the mail. May not sound like much today, but back yonder it was a heap of money. Well, Pa and Harrison had done worked like dogs getting them horses ready. Fine-looking horses, too. Ma didn't trust them fellows, said they had shifty eyes.

"Pa did get a promissory note from 'em. But when all the checking was done, it wasn't worth the paper it was wrote on. The high sheriff was one of Pa's customers, and he'd checked it all out. The army was still waiting on Pa to get the horses ready. Those bad men had done stole the horses, all right, over one hundred head. Pa sat down on the front porch and cried. He'd been through so much, poor Pa. He never was the same after that." This part of the story left all of us with watery eyes.

"Pa said that land was wealth, and wealth meant power, and power ain't got no color," Uncle Porter said. "That's what he taught us, and that's what we're supposed to teach y'all."

Harrison Barrett provided a school and saw to the teaching of his children. He donated the land for the school and the church. All the children knew how to read, write, add, subtract, multiply, and divide. Before he died, Grandfather Harrison drew up a will for the orderly dis-

pensation of his hard-earned goods and proper-
ties.

The old Barrett homestead, with the plants,
trees, and rose bushes brought from slavery
times, is where my father, Eddie (the youngest
of Grandfather Harrison's children) married my
mother, Suwillow Langford. My father reared
me and my siblings in the same traditions and
lessons his father and mother had given him.

In the warm summer weather, Harrison
Barrett's grandchildren would go swimming in
the bubbling waters of the gully and quench
their thirst with the cool, sparkling water from
the freshwater spring. Today that water is
gone, the creek bed covered up by the new U.S.
90 highway.

Grandfather Harrison's original house
burned at Christmas time in the late 1920s.
Eddie, kinfolk, and the neighbors built a mod-
est replacement house on the site, but it was
moved to the rear of the property. A second,
larger house, was built in the mid-1940s.
Today the house is occupied by our sisters,
Oliva Bernice Knox and Deloris Bell, grandchildren of Harrison Barrett.

Grandfather Barrett died in 1917, Anne
fourteen years later. The land was first divided
among Barrett's brothers and sisters and later
on passed to his children. As time passed,
pieces of it were sold.

A lot of people from Louisiana moved to Texas in the 1930s, and many of them bought land in Barrett. That's how the town grew. The extended Barrett family still owns about one hundred acres there. The original Barrett homestead, at thirteen acres, is the same size as it was in the 1930s. It remains the largest tract of Barrett land still in the family after all these years—just like Grandfather envisioned it. In 1988 the Barrett homestead was named a Texas historical site.

Glossary

buy on time—buy with credit.
come into good play—come in handy.
commotion—a big noise or big fuss about something.
flower bed of ease—an easy time.
galled—vexed.
high falutin'—snooty.
huffily—angrily.
loony—silly, crazy.
plumb—completely.
polly-pop, so-good—punch.
rigamarole—a lot of trouble.
sawhorse—a horse-shaped construction used by
     carpenters.
shake a leg—hurry.
so's—so as.
squabbling—arguing.
taking up—living together without being married.
waylay—hide and wait, and then attack someone
     viciously.